Phonics Focus: long e (ee)

AT THE REEF

BY CHRISTINA EARLEY

ILLUSTRATED BY
ANASTASIA KLECKNER

A Blue Marlin Book

Introduction:

Phonics is the relationship between letters and sounds. It is the foundation for reading words, or decoding. A phonogram is a letter or group of letters that represents a sound. Students who practice phonics and sight words become fluent word readers. Having word fluency allows students to build their comprehension skills and become skilled and confident readers.

Activities:

BEFORE READING

Use your finger to underline the key phonogram in each word in the *Words to Read* list on page 3. Then, read the word. For longer words, look for ways to break the word into smaller parts (double letters, word I know, ending, etc.).

DURING READING

Use sticky notes to annotate for understanding. Write questions, make connections, summarize each page after it is read, or draw an emoji that describes how you felt about different parts.

AFTER READING

Share and discuss your sticky notes with an adult or peer who also read the story.

Key Word/Phonogram: reef

Words to Read:

bee	sees	asleep
beet	breeze	beetles
Deen	cheeks	between
deep	cheese	fifteen
eel	green	seaweed
feels	queen	treetop
feet	sheep	weekend
geese	speed	chickadee
jeep	street	needlefish
reef	three	parakeet
reel	tree	

CORAL
REEF

It's the weekend. Deen decides to go to the coral reef.

He drives his jeep with speed. He sees a chickadee and a parakeet in a treetop.

Oh, no! Look out for the sheep and geese in the street!

Deen arrives at Queen Beach.

The tree is a good place to put his green backpack.

The breeze feels nice on the cheeks of his face.

Deen puts his swim fins on his feet.

He puts on his mask and snorkel.

He sees three beetles on line from a fishing reel.

Deen dives deep.

There is a fish that looks like a bee!

An eel swims between the coral.

Deen sees fifteen needlefish in the seaweed.

After snorkeling, Deen feels hungry. He eats his beet and cheese salad for a snack.

He falls asleep under the tree.

Quiz:

1. True or false? Deen sees two kinds of birds in a tree.
2. True or false? Deen puts on his fins before his mask and snorkel.
3. True or false? There is a sea turtle swimming by the coral.
4. Why do you think Deen goes to the coral reef?
5. Where do you think Deen lives? What details in the story support your answer?

Flip the book around for answers!

Answers:

1. True
2. True
3. False
4. Possible answers: He likes to see the fish. Snorkeling is relaxing.
5. Possible answers: Florida, Hawaii. Supporting details: beach with palm trees, coral reef, types of fish.

Activities:

1. Write a story about what happens after Deen wakes up from his nap.
2. Write a new story using some or all of the "ee" words from this book.
3. Create a vocabulary word map for a word that was new to you. Write the word in the middle of a paper. Surround it with a definition, illustration, sentence, and other words related to the vocabulary word.
4. Make a song to help others learn the long e sound of "ee."
5. Design a game to practice reading and spelling words with "ee."

Written by: Christina Earley
Illustrated by: Anastasia Kleckner
Design by: Rhea Magaro-Wallace
Editor: Kim Thompson
Educational Consultant: Marie Lemke, M.Ed.
Series Development: James Earley

Library of Congress PCN Data
At the Reef (ee) / Christina Earley
Blue Marlin Readers
ISBN 978-1-6389-7995-1 (hard cover)
ISBN 979-8-8873-5054-7 (paperback)
ISBN 979-8-8873-5113-1 (EPUB)
ISBN 979-8-8873-5172-8 (eBook)
Library of Congress Control Number: 2022944983

Printed in China.

Seahorse Publishing Company
seahorsepub.com

Published in the United States
Seahorse Publishing
PO Box 771325
Coral Springs, FL 33077